I0086704

Sun-Up, and Other Poems

An Anthology of Political Verse

By Lola Ridge

PANTIANOS
CLASSICS

Published by Pantianos Classics

ISBN-13: 978-1-78987-638-3

First published in 1920

Contents

Dedication

(To my Mother)

Let me cradle myself back
Into the darkness
Of the half shapes...
Of the cauled beginnings...
Let me stir the attar of unused air,
Elusive...ironically fragrant
As a dead queen's kerchief...
Let me blow the dust from off you...
Resurrect your breath
Lying limp as a fan
In a dead queen's hand

Thanks is due to *The New Republic, Poetry, a Magazine of Verse, Play-Boy,* and *Others* for permission to reprint some of these poems.

I - Sun-Up

(Shadows over a cradle...
fire-light craning....
A hand
throws something in the fire
and a smaller hand
runs into the flame and out again,
singed and empty....
Shadows
settling over a cradle...
two hands
and a fire.)

I - Celia

Cherry, cherry,
glowing on the hearth,
bright red cherry....
When you try to pick up cherry
Celia's shriek
sticks in you like a pin.

--

When God throws hailstones
you cuddle in Celia's shawl
and press your feet on her belly
high up like a stool.
When Celia makes umbrella of her hand.
Rain falls through
big pink spokes of her fingers.
When wind blows Celia's gown up off her legs
she runs under pillars of the bank
great round pillars of the bank
have on white stockings too.

--

Celia says my father
will bring me a golden bowl.
When I think of my father
I cannot see him
for the big yellow bowl
like the moon with two handles
he carries in front of him.

--

Grandpa, grandpa…
(Light all about you…
ginger…pouring out of green jars…)
You don't believe he has gone away and left his great coat…
so you pretend…you see his face up in the ceiling.
When you clap your hands and cry, grandpa, grandpa, grandpa,
Celia crosses herself.

--

It isn't a dream....
It comes again and again....
You hear ivy crying on steeples
the flames haven't caught yet
and images screaming
when they see red light on the lilies
on the stained glass window of St. Joseph.
The girl with the black eyes holds you tight,
and you run...and run
past the wild, wild towers…
and trees in the gardens tugging at their feet
and little frightened dolls
shut up in the shops
crying...and crying...because no one stops...
you spin like a penny thrown out in the street.
Then the man clutches her by the hair....
He always clutches her by the hair....
His eyes stick out like spears.
You see her pulled-back face
and her black, black eyes
lit up by the glare....
Then everything goes out.
Please God, don't let me dream any more
of the girl with the black, black eyes.

--

Celia's shadow rocks and rocks…
and mama's eyes stare out of the pillow
as though she had gone away
and the night had come in her place
as it comes in empty rooms…
you can't bear it
the night threshing about
and lashing its tail on its sides
as bold as a wolf that isn't afraid
and you scream at her face, that is white as a stone on a
    grave
and pull it around to the light,

7

till the night draws backward...the night that walks
    alone
and goes away without end.
Mama says, I am cold, Betty, and shivers.
Celia tucks the quilt about her feet,
but I run for my little red cloak
because red is hot like fire.

                     --

I wish Celia
could see the sea climb up on the sky
and slide off again..
...*Celia saying*
I'd beg the world with you....
Celia...holding on to the cab...
hands wrenched away..
wind in the masts...like Celia crying....
Celia never minded if you slapped her
when the comb made your hairs ache,
but though you rub your cheek against mama's hand
she has not said darling since....
Now I will slap her again....
I will bite her hand till it bleeds.

It is cool by the port hole.
The wet rags of the wind
flap in your face.

II - The Alley

Because you are four years old
the candle is all dressed up in a new frill.
And stars nod to you through the hole in the curtain,
(except the big stiff planets
too fat to move about much,)
and you curtsey back to the stars
when no one is looking.
You feel sorry for the poor wooden chair
that knows it isn't nice to sit on,
and no one is sad but mama.
You don't like mama to be sad
when you are four years old,
so you pretend
you like the bitter gold-pale tea -
you pretend

if you don't drink it up pretty quick
a little gold-fish
will think it is a pond
and come and get born in it.

--

It's hot in our street
and the breeze is a dirty little broom
that sweeps dust into our room
and bits of paper out of the alley.
You are not let to play
with the children in the alley
But you must be very polite
so you pass them and say good day
and when they fling banana skins
you fling them back again.

--

There is no one to play with
and the flies on the window
buzz and buzz…
…you can pull out their legs
and stick pins in their bodies
but still they buzz…
and mama says:
When Nero was a little boy
he caught flies on his mama's window
and pulled out their legs
and stuck pins in their bodies
and nobody loved him.
Buzz, blue-bellied flies -
buzz, nasty black wheel
of mama's machine -
you are the biggest fly of all -
you have the loudest buzz.
I hear you at dawn before the locusts.
But I like the picture of the Flood
and the little babies getting drowned…
If I were there I would save them,
but as I can't save them
I like to watch them
getting drowned.

--

When mama buys of Ling Ho,
he smiles very wide
and picks her the largest loquots.
The greens-man gave her a cabbage

9

and she held it against her black bodice
and said what a beautiful green it was
and put it on the table
as though it had been a flower.
But next day we boiled and ate it with salt.
It was our dinner.

--

Christmas day
I found Janie on my pillow.
Janie is made of rubber.
Her red and blue jacket won't come off.
Christmas dinner was green and white
chicken and lettuce and peas
and drops of oil on the salad
smiley and full of light
like the gold on the lady's teeth.
But mama said politely
Thank you, we are dining out.
She wouldn't let you take one pea
to put in the hole where the whistle was
at the back of Janie's head,
so Janie should have some dinner
So you went to the park with biscuits
and black tea in a bottle.

--

You feel very sad
when you climb on the fence
to watch mama out of sight.
The women in the alley
poke their heads out of doorways
and watch her too.
You know her
by the way she holds her shoulders
till she is only a speck -
in a chain of specks
till she is swallowed up.
But suppose
that day after day
you were to watch for her face
and it didn't come back?
Suppose
it were to drop out of the string of white faces
like the pearl out of my chain
I never found again?
Mabel minds you while mama is out,

she washes while she sings
Three blind mice!
they all run away from the farmer's wife
who cut off their tails
with a carving knife -
Wind blows out Mabel's sheets,
way you blow in a bag before you burst it.
Wind has a soapy smell.
It's heavier n sun
that lies all over you without any weight
and makes you feel happy
and crinkly like bubbling water.
There's no sun on the empty house -
sly-looking house -
you can't see in its windows
that watch you out of their corners.
Perhaps there's a big spider there
spinning gray threads over the windows
till they look like dead people's faces....
Jimmie says:
Jimmie's hair is white as a white mouse.
His lashes are gold as mama's wedding ring
and his mouth feels cool and smooth
like a flower wet with rain.
You wouldn't believe Jimmie was different...till he
showed you....

                              --

Blind wet sheets
flapping on the lines...
sun in your eyes,
dark gold sun
full of little black spots,
you have to blink and blink...
round eyes of Jimmie....
Jimmie's blue jumper...
blue shadow of wall...
all the world holding still
as when a clock stops...
streets still...people still...
no streets... no people...
only sky and wall...
sun glaring bright as God
down at you and Jimmie...
shadow like a purple cloth
trailing off the wall...

Wild wet sheets
flapping in the wind...
big slippered feet flapping too...
big-balloon-face
rushing up the alley...
houses closing up again...
windows looking round...
...Mabel pulls you in the gate and shakes you
and tells you not to tell your mama...
And you wonder
if God has spoiled Jimmie.

III - Mama

Mama's face
is smooth and pale as tea-rose leaves.
That ivory oval of aunt Gem
you sucked the miniature off
had black black hair like mama.

--

Pit-it-ty-pat,
Mama walks so fast,
street lamps jig
without bending a leg...
lights in the windows
play twinkling tunes
on crimson and blue
bottles like bubbles
big as balloons...
Faster and faster...
and pink light spurts
over cakes doing polkas
in little white shirts,
with cake-princesses
in flounced white skirts.
Pit-pat -
mama walks slower...
slower and...slower....
Eyes...lamps...stars . .
acres and acres of stars...
bells...and sleepily
flapping feet....
You re glad mama walks slow.
It's nice to be carried along

up high near the stars
that look at you with a grave, great look.
                              --

Every night
mama sings you to sleep.
When she sings, *O for the light of thine eyes Dolores,*
there's a castle on a cliff
and the sea roars like lions.
It leaps at the castle
and the cliff knocks it down
but always the sea
shakes its flattened head
and gets up again.
The castle has no roof
so the rain spins silvery webs in it,
and Dolores face
floats dim and beautiful
the way flowers do when they are drowned.
Step by white step
she goes up the castle stairs,
but the stair goes up into the sky
and the sky keeps going up too,
so none of them ever get there.

When mama sings *Ba ba black sheep,*
the stars seem to shine through her voice
so everything has to be still,
and when she has finished singing
her song goes up off the earth,
higher and higher...
till it is only as big as a tiny silver bird
with nothing but moonlight around it.

IV - Betty

You can see the sandhills from our new room.
Butterflies
live in the sandhills
and lizards
and centipedes.
If you keep very still
lizards will think you a stone
and run over your lap.
Butterflies liveries
are scarlet and black.

They drive chariots in air.
People in the chariots
are pale as dew -
you can see right through them -
but the chariots
are made of gold of the sun.
They go up to heaven
and never catch fire.
There are green centipedes
and brown centipedes
and black centipedes,
because green and brown and black
are the colors in hell's flag.
Centipedes
have hundreds of feet
because it is so far from hell
to come up for air.
Centipedes
do not hurry.
They are waiting for the last day
when they will creep over the false prophets
who will have their hands tied.

--

Night calls to the sandhills
and gathers them under her.
she pushes away cities
because their sharp lights
hurt her soft breast.
Even candles make a sore place
when they stick in the night.

There are things in the sandhills
that no one knows about...
they come out at dark when the young snakes play
and tell each other secrets
in the deaf logs.

Sometimes...before rain...
when the stars have gone inside...
the night comes close to your window
and sniffs at the light....
But you must not run away
you must keep your face to the night
and walk backward.

--

When it rains
and you are pulling off flies legs...
mama lets you play houses
with Lizzie and Clara.
Because you are the Only One
and because Only Ones have to live alone
while sisters stay together,
Lizzie and Clara
give you the dry house
and take the one with the leaking roof.

Rain like curly hairpins
blows on Lizzie and Clara's two heads
turned like one head -
two mouths
spread into one laugh.
Lizzie is saying:
why don't you want to play -
when you feel you'd like to braid
the crinkled-silver rain
into a shining rope
to climb up... and up... and up... into the
      wet sky
and never see any one again.

Our gate doesn't hang right.
It must have pawed at the wind
and gotten a kick
as the wind passed over.
The sitting sky
puffs out a gray smoke
and the wind makes a red-striped sound
blowing out straight,
but our gate drags its foot
and whines to itself on one hinge.

--

What do you think I've found
two wee knockers of fairy brass,
or two gold sovereigns folded up
in a bit of green silk,
or two gold bugs
in little green shirts?
If you want to know,
you must walk tip-toe
so your feet just whisper in the grass -

15

you must carry them careful
and very proud,
for their stems bleed drops of milk -
but Lizzie and Clara shout in glee:
Pee-a-bed, pee-a-bed -
dandelions!
You look in the eyes of grown-up people
to see if they feel
the way you feel...
but they hide inside of themselves,
and so you do not find out.
Grown-up people say:
The stars are bright to-night,
but they do not say
what you are thinking about stars -
not even mama says what you are thinking about stars.
This makes you feel very lonely.

--

It's strange about stars....
You have to be still when they look at you.
They push your song inside of you with their song.
Their long silvery rays
sink into you and do not hurt.
It is good to feel them resting on you
like great white birds...
and their shining whiteness
doesn't burn like the sun -
it washes all over you
and makes you feel cleaner'n water.

--

My doll Janie has no waist
and her body is like a tub with feet on it.
Sometimes I beat her
but I always kiss her afterwards.
When I have kissed all the paint off her body
I shall tie a ribbon about it
so she shan't look shabby.
But it must be blue -
it mustn't be pink -
pink shows the dirt on her face
that won't wash off.

--

I beat Janie
and beat her...
but still she smiled...

so I scratched her between the eyes with a pin.
Now she doesn't love me any more...
she scowls...and scowls...
though I've begged her to forgive me
and poured sugar in the hole at the back of her head.

--

Mama says Janie is a fairy doll
and she *has* forgiven me
that she's gone to the market
to buy me some sweets.
- Now she's at the door
and a little bag tied to her neck -
I run to Janie
and kiss her all over....
Ah... she is still frowning.
I let the sweets drop on the floor
mama
has told you a lie.

--

Chinaman
singing in street:
gleen ledd-ish-es, gleen ledd-ish-es -
hot sun
shining on your face
it must be a new day.
But why aren't you happy
if it's a new day?
Because something has happened...
something sad and terrible....
Now I remember...it's Janie.
Yesterday
I took Janie out
and tied my handkerchief over her face
and put sand in it
and threw her into the ditch
down in the black water
under the dock leaves...
and when mama asked me where Janie was
I said I had lost her.

--

I'm glad it is night-time
so I'll be able to go to sleep
and forget all about it....
But mama looks at my tongue
and says she will give me senna tea.

17

When you smell the tea
you shut your eyes tight
and pretend not to hear
the soft, cool voice of mama
that goes over your forehead
like a little wind.
And then you lie in the dark
and stare...and stare...
till the faces come...
yellow faces with leering eyes
drifting in a greeny mist....
I wonder
if Janie sees faces
out there...alone in the dark....
I wonder
if she has got the handkerchief off
or if the water has gone in the hole
where the whistle was
at the back of her head
and drowned her...
or if the stars
can see her under the dock leaves?

--

It's smoky-blue and still
over the red road.
Wind must be lying down with its tail under it -
doesn't even flick off the flies.
And you can hear the silence
buzzing in the gum trees,
the way the angels buzzed
when they flew through the cedars of Lebanon
with thin gauze wings
you could see through.
Nice to hear the silence buzzing -
till it comes too close
and booms in your ears
and presses all over you
till you scream....
When you scream at the silence
it goes to jingling pieces
like a silver mirror
broken into tiny bits.
Perhaps its wings are made of glass -
perhaps it lives down in a dark, dark cave
and only comes up

to warm its wings in the sun....
It's cold in the cave -
no matter how you cover yourself up.
Little girls sit there
dressed in white
and the dolls in their arms
all have white handkerchiefs
over their faces.
Their shadows cannot play with them...
their shadows lie down at their feet...
for the little girls sit stiff as stones
with their backs to the mouth of the cave
where a little light falls off
the wings of the silence
when it comes down out of the sun.

--

Moon catches the flying fish
as they dive in the bay.
Flying fish
spin over and over
slippity-silver
into the water.
Moon bends over jungles
and touches the foreheads of tigers
as they pass under openings made by dropped leaves.
Tigers stop on the trail of the deer
while the moon is on their foreheads -
they let the stags go by.

Moon is shining strangely
on the white palings of the fence.
Fence keeps very still...
most times it moves a little...
everything moves a little
though you mayn't know it...
but now the little fence
wouldn't change places with the great cross
that stands so stiff and high
with its back to the moon.
Moon shining strangely
on the white palings of the fence,
I am shining too
but my light is shut inside of me
and can't get out.

--

Old house with black windows -
blind house begging moonlight
to put out the shadows -
why do you want so much light?
You creak when the wind steps on you -
you cough up dust
and your beams ache -
you know you will soon fall,
the moon just pities you!
Don't waste yourself moon -
come on my bed and play with me.
Wrap me up in blue light,
you who are cool.
I am too hot,
I am all alive
and the shadows are outside of me.

--

There are different kinds of shadows.
The blind ones
are the shadows of things.
These are the tame shadows -
they love to play on the wall with you
and follow you about like cats and dogs.
Sometimes
they hiss at you softly
like snakes that do not bite,
or swish like women's dresses,
but if you poke a candle at them
they pull in their heads and disappear.

But there is a shadow
that is not the shadow of a thing...
it is a thing itself.
When you meet this shadow
you must not look at it too long...
it grows with your looking at it...
till you are all alone
with nothing around you...
nothing...nothing...nothing...
but a shadow
with its eyes full of black light.

--

There's a shadow in the corner of the shed,
crouching, lying in wait...
a black coiled shadow,

watching...ready to strike...
but I mustn't be afraid of it -
I mustn't be afraid of anything.
Poor evil shadow,
the candle would chase it away
only she can't get at it.
Do you think that every one hates you,
shadow with your back to the wall,
afraid to lie down and sleep?
But I don't hate you.
Even the moon means to be kind.
She just treads on you
as I'd tread on a worm that I didn't see.
Don't be afraid of me, shadow.
See - I've no light in my hand -
nothing to save myself with -
yet I walk right up to you -
if you'll let me
I'll put my arms around you
and stroke you softly.
Are you surprised I'd put my arms around you?
Is it your black black sorrow
that nobody loves you?

V - Jude

When you tell mama
you are going to do something great
she looks at you
as though you were a window
she were trying to see through,
and says she hopes you will be good
instead of great.

--

When you are five years old
you spend the day in the Gardens.
The grass is greener than cabbages,
and orange lilies
stand up very straight
and will not curtsey to the sun
when the wind tells them.
Only pansies bow down very low.
Pansies make little purple cushions
for queen bees to stand on.

21

Bees
have brown silk hair on their bodies.
If you are careful
they will let you stroke them.

The trees over the marble man
catch up all the sunbeams
so the shadows have it their way -
the shadows swallow him up
like a blue shark.
When you scoop a sunbeam up on your palm
and offer it to the marble man,
he does not notice...
he looks into his stone beard.
...When you do something great
people give you a stone face,
so you do not care any more
when the sun throws gold on you
through leaf -holes the wind makes
in green bushes....
This thought makes me very sad.

--

Jude has eyes like tobacco
with yellow specks on it
and his hair is red as a red orange.
Jude and I
have made a garden in the field
that no one knows about.
We creep in and out
through a little place
where the barbed wire is down.
We lie in the long grass
and crush dandelions
between our two cheeks
till their milk comes out on our faces.
We hold each other tight
and the wind tip-toes all over us
and pelts us with thistle-down.

--

Jude isn't afraid of shadows -
not even of the ones that have eyes in them.
And he can look in the face of the sun
without blinking at all.
Hush! don't say *sun* so loud.
The sun gets angry when you stare at him.

If you peek in his glory-windows
he spreads into a great white flame
like God out of his Burning Bush...
till you put your hands up on your face
and tremble like a drop of rain upon a flower
that some one throws into the fire...
and then
the sun makes himself small,
the sun swings down out of the sky -
littler n a star,
little as a spark
little as a fierce red spider
on a burning thread...
and then
the light goes out...
shivers into blackened bits....
You hold on to a wall that whirls around
and the gate is a black hole.
You grope your way in like a toad
that's blinded by a stone...
and mama puts on cold wet rags
that get hot soon....
Hush! don't let's talk about the sun.

--

When you pass by the ditch where Janie is
You run very fast
and look at the other side.
Jude says Janie did love me
only she couldn't forgive me,
and that you can love people very much
and never, never, never forgive them....
so we poked a stick in the bottle-green water.
But only weeds came up
and an old top with the paint washed off.

--

Jude and I
wave to the new moon
curled right up like one gold hair
on the bald-head sandhill.
Mama peeps out the window and smiles.
She thinks
I am playing with myself...
Run, Jude, run with the wind -
but hold my hand tight
or the wind,

23

looking for some one to play with,
will take me away from you!
Wind with no one to play with
cooees the orange-trees -
stay-at-home orange trees,
have to nurse oranges,
greeny-gold.
Wind shouts to the grass -
run-away-grass
tugs at its roots,
but the earth holds tight
and the grass falls down
and wind boos over it.
Wind whistles the bees -
bees too busy
with taking home stuff out of flowers
won't look back -
bees always going somewhere.
Only Jude and I -
heads over shoulders
watching all roads at one time -
run with the wind,
going to nowhere.

                                    --

Jude and I
were weeding our garden
when we heard his whip
must have been a new whip -
to cut off dandelion-heads at one swing...
He was the kind of boy you knew when you had Celia...
with nice clothes on and curls
crawling about his collar
like little golden slugs,
and his man was leading his horse.
I wish I hadn't run to meet him...
If you hadn't run to meet him
he mightn't have trod on your garden and said:
Get out of my field you dirty little beggar...
he mightn't have struck you with his whip....
How the daisies stared...
I hate daisies -
stupid white faces -
skinny necks
craning over the grass!
I said It is not your field,

and he struck me again.
But he didn't make me run.
His hand
smelled of sweet soap...
he couldn't shake me off,
but his man did....
Funny - how the sky fell down
and turned over and over
like a blue carpet rolling you up,
and the grass caught at your face -
it couldn't have been spiteful -
it must have been saving itself.
Hot road...silly wind playing with your hair...
The road smelled of horses.
I only got up
when I heard a dray.

--

Mama has sung ba ba black sheep,
and put a chair with a cloth on it
between me and the light.
But the clock keeps saying:
Dirty little beggar,
dirty little beggar....
Some day
I will get that boy.
I will pull off his arms and legs
and put him in a box
and hide the box
under the bed....
I wonder
will he buzz
when I take him out to look at his body
that will have no arms to whip me?

Mama drew my cot to the window
so I can look at the stars.
I will not look at the stars.
There is a black chimney
throwing up sparks
and one tall flame
like gold hair in a blaze....
I know now
what I shall do....
I will set fire to him
and he will burn up into a tall flame -

he will scream into the sky
and sparks will fly out of him -
he will burn and burn...
and his blazing hair
shall light up the world.

--

Before he hit me -
I knew he was going to -
I thought about Jude....
I thought if he'd fight...
but he shriveled all up...
he lay down like a fear.

Mama never knew about Jude.
You always wanted to tell her,
but somehow you never did.
You were afraid she'd smile
and say he wasn't real -
that he was only a little dream-boy,
because the grass didn't fall down under his feet.
He is fading now....
He is just lines...like a drawing....
You can see mama in between.
When she moves
she rubs some of him out.

Monologues

Jaguar

Nasal intonations of light
and clicking tongues...
publicity of windows
stoning me with pent-up cries...
smells of abattoirs...
smells of long-dead meat.

Some day-end -
while the sand is yet cozy as a blanket
off the warm body of a squaw,
and the jaguars are out to kill...
with a blue-black night coming on
and a painted cloud
stalking the first star -
I shall go alone into the Silence...
the coiled Silence...
where a cry can run only a little way
and waver and dwindle
and be lost.

And there...
where tiny antlers clinch and strain
as life grapples in a million avid points,
and threshing things
strike and die,
letting their hate live on
in the spreading purple of a wound...
I too
will make covert of a crevice in the night,
and turn and watch...
nose at the cleft's edge.

Wild Duck

I

That was a great night we spied upon
See-sawing home,
Singing a hot sweet song to the super-stars
Shuffling off behind the smoke-haze...
Fog-horns sentimentalizing on the river...
Lights dwindling to shining slits
In the wet asphalt...
Purring lights...red and green and golden-whiskered...
Digging daintily pointed claws in the soft mud...
...But you did not know...
As the trains made golden augers
Boring in the darkness...
How my heart kept racing out along the rails,
As a spider runs along a thread
And hauls him in again
To some drawing point...
You did not know
How wild ducks wings
Itch at ctawn...
How at dawn the necks of wild ducks
Arch to the sun
And new-mown air
Trickles sweet in their gullets.

II

As water, cleared of the reflection of a bird
That has lately flown across it,
Yet trembles with the beating of its wings,
So my soul...emptied of the known you... utterly...
Is yet vibrant with the cadence of the song
You might have been....
'Twas a great night...
With never a waste look over a shoulder
Curved to the crook of the wind...
And a great word we threw
For memory to play knuckles with...
A word the waters of the world have washed,
Leaving it stark and without smell...
A world that rattles well in emptiness:
    Good-by.

The Dream

I have a dream
to fill the golden sheath
of a remembered day....
(Air
heavy and massed and blue
as the vapor of opium...
domes
fired in sulphurous mist...
sea
quiescent as a gray seal...
and the emerging sun
spurting up gold
over Sydney, smoke-pale, rising out of the bay....)
But the day is an up-turned cup
and its sun a junk of red iron
guttering in sluggish-green water -
where shall I pour my dream?

Altitude

I WONDER
how it would be here with you,
where the wind
that has shaken off its dust in low valleys
touches one cleanly,
as with a new-washed hand,
and pain
is as the remote hunger of droning things,
and anger
but a little silence
sinking into the great silence.

Comrades

Life
You have been good to me....
You have not made yourself too dear
to juggle with.

Nocturne

Indigo bulb of darkness
Punctured by needle lights
Through a fissure of brick canyon
    shutting out stars,
And a sliver of moon
Spigoting two high windows
    over the West river....

Boy, I met to-night,
Your eyes are two red-glowing arcs
shifting with my vision....
They reflect as in a fading proof
The deadened eyes of a woman,
And your shed virginity,
Light as the withered pod of a sweet pea,
Moist and fragrant
Blows against my soul.
What are you to me, boy,
That I, who have passed so many lights,
Should carry your eyes
Like swinging lanterns?

Cactus Seed

I

Radiant notes
piercing my narrow-chested room,
beating down through my ceiling -
smeared with unshapen
belly-prints of dreams
drifted out of old smokes -
trillions of icily
peltering notes
out of just one canary,
all grown to song
as a plant to its stalk,
from too long craning at a sky-light
and a square of second-hand blue.

Silvery-strident throat -
so assiduously serenading my brain,
flinching under

30

the glittering hail of your notes -
were you not safe behind...rats know what thickness
      of... plastered wall...
I might fathom
your golden delirium
with throttle of finger and thumb
shutting valve of bright song.

II

But if... away off... on a fork of grassed earth
socketing an inlet reach of blue water...
if canaries (do they sing out of cages?)
flung such luminous notes,
they would sink in the spirit...
lie germinal...
housed in the soul as a seed in the earth...
to break forth at spring with the crocuses
      into young smiles on the mouth.
Or glancing off buoyantly,
radiate notes in one key
with the sparkle of rain-drops
on the petal of a cactus flower
focusing the just-out sun.

Cactus...why cactus?
God...God...
somewhere...away off...
cactus flowers, star-yellow
ray out of spiked green,
and empties of sky
roll you over and over
like a mother her baby in long grass.
And only the wind scandal-mongers with gum trees,
pricking multiple leaves
at his amazing story.

Windows

Time-Stone

Hallo, Metropolitan -
Ubiquitous windows staring all ways,
Red eye notching the darkness.
No use to ogle that slip of a moon.
This midnight the moon,
Playing virgin after all her encounters,
Will break another date with you.
You fuss an awful lot,
You flight of ledger books,
Overrun with multiple ant-black figures
Dancing on spindle legs
An interminable can-can.
But I'd rather...like the cats in the alley
    count time
By the silver whistle of a moonbeam
Falling between my stoop-shouldered walls,
Than all your tally of the sunsets,
Metropolitan, ticking among stars.

Train Window

Small towns
Crawling out of their green shirts...
Tubercular towns
Coughing a little in the dawn...
And the church...
There is always a church
With its natty spire
And the vestibule -
That's where they whisper:
Tzz-tzz...tzz-tzz...tzz-tzz...
How many codes for a wireless whisper -
And corn flatter than it should be
And those chits of leaves
Gadding with every wind?
Small towns
From Connecticut to Maine:
Tzz-tzz . . tzz-tzz . . tzz-tzz. ,

32

Scandal

AREN'T there bigger things to talk about
Than a window in Greenwich Village
And hyacinths sprouting
Like little puce poems out of a sick soul?
Some cosmic hearsay -
As to whom - it can't be Mars!
   put the moon - *that way*....
Or what winds do to canyons
Under the tall stars...
Or even
How that old roue, Neptune,
Cranes over his bald-head moons
At the twinkling heel of a sky-scraper.

Electricity

Out of fiery contacts...
Rushing auras of steel
Touching and whirled apart
Out of the charged phallases
Of iron leaping
Female and male,
Complete, indivisible, one,
Fused into light.

Skyscrapers

Skyscrapers...remote, unpartisan...
Turning neither to the right nor left
Your imperturbable fronts....
Austerely greeting the sun
With one chilly finger of stone....
I know your secrets...better than all the policemen
   like fat blue mullet along the avenues.

Wall Street at Night

Long vast shapes...cooled and flushed through with darkness....
Lidless windows
Glazed with a flashy luster
From some little pert cafe chirping up like a sparrow.
And down among iron guts
Piled silver
Throwing gray spatter of light...pale without heat...
Like the pallor of dead bodies.

East River

Dour river
Jaded with monotony of lights
Diving off mast heads....
Lights mad with creating in a river...turning its sullen back....
Heave up, river...
Vomit back into the darkness your spawn of light...
The night will gut what you give her.

Secrets

Interim

The earth is motionless
And poised in space...
A great bird resting in its flight
Between the alleys of the stars.
It is the wind's hour off...
The wind has nestled down among the corn...
The two speak privately together,
Awaiting the whirr of wings.

After Storm

Was there a wind?
Tap...tap....
Night pads upon the snow
with moccasined feet...
and it is still...so still...
an eagle's feather
might fall like a stone.
Could there have been a storm...
mad-tossing golden mane on the neck of the wind
tearing up the sky...
loose-flapping like a tent
about the ice-capped stars?

Cool, sheer and motionless
the frosted pines
are jeweled with a million flaming points
that fling their beauty up in long white sheaves
till they catch hands with stars.
Could there have been a wind
that haled them by the hair....
and blinding
blue-forked
flowers of the lightning
in their leaves?
Tap...tap...
slow-ticking centuries...

Soft as bare feet upon the snow
faint...lulling as heard rain
upon heaped leaves....
Silence
builds her wall
about a dream impaled.

Secrets

Secrets
infesting my half-sleep...
did you enter my wound from another wound
brushing mine in a crowd...
or did I snare you on my sharper edges
as a bird flying through cobwebbed trees at sun-up
carries off spiders on its wings?

Secrets,
running over my soul without sound,
only when dawn comes tip-toeing
ushered by a suave wind,
and dreams disintegrate
like breath shapes in frosty air,
I shall overhear you, bare-foot,
scatting off into the darkness....
I shall know you, secrets
by the litter you have left
and by your bloody foot-prints.

Potpourri

Do you remember
Honey-melon moon
Dripping thick sweet light
Where Canal Street saunters off by herself
        among quiet trees?
And the faint decayed patchouli -
Fragrance of New Orleans
Like a dead tube rose
Upheld in the warm air...
Miraculously whole.

Thaw

Blow through me wind
As you blow through apple blossoms....
Scatter me in shining petals over the passers-by...
Joyously I reunite...sway and gather to myself...
Sedately I walk by the dancing feet of children -
Not knowing I too dance over the cobbled spring.
O, but they laugh back at me,
(Eyes like daisies smiling wide open),
And we both look askance at the snowed-in people
Thinking me one of them.

Portraits

Mother

I

Your love was like moonlight
turning harsh things to beauty,
so that little wry souls
reflecting each other obliquely
as in cracked mirrors...
beheld in your luminous spirit
their own reflection,
transfigured as in a shining stream,
and loved you for what they are not.

You are less an image in my mind
than a luster
I see you in gleams
pale as star-light on a gray wall...
evanescent as the reflection of a white swan
shimmering in broken water.

II

(To E. S.)

You inevitable,
Unwieldy with enormous births,
Lying on your back, eyes open, sucking down stars,
Or you kissing and picking over fresh deaths...
Filth...worms...flowers...
Green and succulent pods...
Tremulous gestation
Of dark water germinal with lilies...
All in you from the beginning...
Nothing buried or thrown away...
Only the moon like a white sheet
Spread over the dead you carry.

III

(To H.)

Speeding gull
Passing under a cloud
Caught on his white back
You...drop of crystal rain.
Now you gleam softly triumphant
Folding immensities of light.

IV

(To O. F. T.)

You have always gotten up after blows
And smiled...and shaken off the dust...
Only you could not shake the darkness
From off the bruised brown of your eyes.

V

(To E. A. R.)

Centuries shall not deflect
nor many suns
absorb your stream,
flowing immune and cold
between the banks of snow.
Nor any wind
carry the dust of cities
to your high waters
that arise out of the peaks
and return again into the mountain
and never descend.

Sons of Belial

We are old,
Old as song.
Before Rome was
Or Cyrene.
Mad nights knew us
And old men's wives.
We knew who spilled the sacred oil
For young-gold harlots of the town…
We knew where the peacocks went
And the white doe for sacrifice.

II

We were the sons of Belial.
One black night
Centuries ago
We beat at a door
In Gilead....
We took the Levite's concubine
We plucked her hands from off the door…
We choked the cry into her throat
And stuck the stars among her hair...
We glimpsed the madly swaying stars
Between the rhythms of her hair...
And all our mute and separate strings
Swelled in a raging symphony....
Our blood sang paeans
All that night
Till dawn fell like a wounded swan
Upon the fields of Gilead.

III

We are old....
Old as song....
We are dumb song.

(Epics tingled
In our blood
When we haled Hypatia
Over the stones
In Alexandria.)

Could we loose
The wild rhythms clinched in us…
March in bands of troubadours…
We would be of gentle mood.
When Christ healed us
Who were dumb -
When he freed our shut-in song -
We strewed green palms
At his pale feet...
We sang hosannas
In Jerusalem.
And all our fumbling voices blent
In a brief white harmony.
(But a mightier song
Was in us pent
When we nailed Christ
To a four-armed tree.)

IV

We are young.
When we rise up with singing roots,
(Warm rains washing
Gutters of Berlin
Where we stamped Rosa...Luxemburg
On a night in spring.)
Rhythms skurry in our blood.
Little nimble rats of song
In our feet run crazily
And all is dust...we trample...on.

Mad nights when we make ritual
(Feet running before the sleuth-light…
And the smell of burnt flesh
By a flame-ringed hut
In Missouri,
Sweet as on Rome's pyre....)
We make ropes do rigadoons
With copper feet that jig on air...

We are the Mob…
Old as song.
Tyre knew us
And Israel.

Reveille

In Harness

The foreman's head
slowly circling...
White rims
under yellow disks of eyes....
Gold hairs
starting out of a blond scowl...
Hovering...disappearing...recurring
the foreman's head.

Droning of power-machines...
droning of girl with adenoids...
Arms flapping with a fin-like motion
under sun burning down through a sky-light
     like a glass lid.
Light skating on the rims of wheels...
boring in gimlet points.
Needles flickering
fierce white threads of light
fine as a wasp's sting.
Light in sweat-drops brighter than eyes
and calico-pallid faces
and bodies throwing off smells -
and the air a bloated presence
     pressing on the walls
and the silence a compressed scream.

Allons enfants de la patrie -
Electric...piercing...shrill as a fife
the voice of a little Russian
breaks out of the shivered circle.
Another voice rises...another and another
leaps like flame to flame.
And life - surging, clamorous, swarming like a rabble
     crazily fluttering ragged petticoats -
comes rushing back into torpid eyes
like suddenly yielded gates.

The girl with adenoids
rocks on her hams.
A torrent of song
strains at her throat,
gurgles, rushes, gouges her blocked pipes.
Her feet beat a wild tattoo -
head flung back and pelvis lifting
to the white body of the sun.
Mates now, these two -
goddess and god....
Marchons!

Only the power machines drone
with metallic docility
under the flaxen head of the foreman
poised like an amazed gull.

II

To-day
little French merchant men
with pointed beards
and fat American merchant men
without any beards
drive to a feast of buttered squabs.
The band...accoutered and neatly caparisoned...
        plays the Marseillaise....
And I think of a wild stallion...newly caught...
flanks yet taut and nostrils spread
to the smell of a racing mare,
hitched to a grocer's cart.

Reveille

Come forth, you workers!
Let the fires go cold -
Let the iron spill out, out of the troughs -
Let the iron run wild
Like a red bramble on the floors -
Leave the mill and the foundry and the mine
And the shrapnel lying on the wharves -
Leave the desk and the shuttle and the loom -

Come,
With your ashen lives,
Your lives like dust in your hands.

I call upon you, workers.
It is not yet light
But I beat upon your doors.
You say you await the Dawn
But I say you are the Dawn.
Come, in your irresistible unspent force
And make new light upon the mountains.

You have turned deaf ears to others -
Me you shall hear.
Out of the mouths of turbines,
Out of the turgid throats of engines,
Over the whistling steam,
You shall hear me shrilly piping.
Your mills I shall enter like the wind,
And blow upon your hearts,
Kindling the slow fire.

They think they have tamed you, workers -
Beaten you to a tool
To scoop up hot honor
Till it be cool -
But out of the passion of the red frontiers
A great flower trembles and burns and glows
And each of its petals is a people.

Come forth, you workers -
Clinging to your stable
And your wisp of warm straw -
Let the fires grow cold,
Let the iron spill out of the troughs,
Let the iron run wild
Like a red bramble on the floors...

As our forefathers stood on the prairies
So let us stand in a ring,
Let us tear up their prisons like grass
And beat them to barricades -
Let us meet the fire of their guns
With a greater fire,
Till the birds shall fly to the mountains
For one safe bough.

To Alexander Berkman

Can you see me, Sasha?
I can see you....
A tentacle of the vast dawn is resting on your face
that floats as though detached
in a sultry and greenish vapor.
I cannot reach my hands to you...
would not if I could,
though I know how warmly yours would close about
    them.
Why?
I do not know...
I have a sense of shame.
Your eyes hurt me...mysterious openings in the gray
    stone of your face
through which your spirit streams out taut as a flag
bearing strange symbols to the new dawn.

If I stay...projected, trembling against these bars filtering emaciated light...
will your eyes...that bore their lonely way through mine...
stop as at a friendly gate...
grow warm...and luminous?
...but I cannot stay...for the smell...
I know...how the days pass...
The prison squats
with granite haunches
on the young spring,
battened under with its twisting green...
and you...socket for every bolt
piercing like a driven nail.
Eyes stare you through the bars...
eyes blank as a graveled yard...
and the silence shuffles heavy dice of feet in iron corridors...
until the day...that has soiled herself in this black
    hole
to caress the pale mask of your face...
withdraws the last wizened ray
to wash in the infinite
her discolored hands.
Can you hear me, Sasha,
in your surrounded darkness?

Emma Goldman

How should they appraise you,
who walk up close to you
as to a mountain,
each proclaiming his own eyeful
against the other's eyeful.

Only time
standing well off
shall measure your circumference
        and height.

An Old Workman

Warped...gland-dry...
With spine askew
And body shrunken into half its space...
Well-used as some cracked paving-stone...
Bearing on his grimed and pitted front
A stamp...as of innumerable feet.

To Larkin

Is it you I see go by the window, Jim Larkin - you not
        looking at me nor any one,
And your shadow swaying from East to West?
Strange that you should be walking free you shut down
        without light,
And your legs tied up with a knot of iron.
One hundred million men and women go inevitably about
        their affairs,
In the somnolent way
Of men before a great drunkenness....
They do not see you go by their windows, Jim Larkin,
With your eyes bloody as the sunset
And your shadow gaunt upon the sky...
You, and the like of you, that life
Is crushing for their frantic wines.

Wind Rising in the Alleys

Wind rising in the alleys
My spirit lifts in you like a banner
   streaming free of hot walls.
You are full of unspent dreams....
You are laden with beginnings....
There is hope in you...not sweet....
   acrid as blood in the mouth.
Come into my tossing dust
Scattering the peace of old deaths,
Wind rising in the alleys,
Carrying stuff of flame.

www.ingramcontent.com/pod-product-compliance
Lightning Source LLC
Chambersburg PA
CBHW031530040426
42445CB00009B/473